Improve your aural!

Paul Harris and John Lenehan

Contents

fabermusic.com

© 2006 by Faber Music Ltd
First published in 2006 by Faber Music Ltd
Bloomsbury House 74–77 Great Russell Street London WC1B 3DA
Music processed by Music Set 2000
Design by Susan Clarke
Illustrations on page 9 by Drew Hillier
Printed in England by Caligraving Ltd
All rights reserved
ISBN10: 0-571-52455-9
EAN13: 978-0-571-52455-6

CD recorded in Rectory Studio, High Wycombe, March 2006
Created and produced by John Lenehan
Thanks to Godstowe School Chamber Choir 2006 and Laurel Hopkinson
℗ 2006 Faber Music Ltd
© 2006 Faber Music Ltd

FABER *ff* MUSIC

Why is aural important?

You may wonder why you have to do aural at all. The answer is, that aural will help you improve as a musician. And this may surprise you – it will help perhaps more than *any other* single musical skill.

Aural is all about understanding and processing music that you hear and see, in your head. By doing so, you will find that your own playing improves enormously. You will be able to play more expressively and stylistically, be more sensitive to quality and control of tone, your music reading will improve, you will be able to spot your own mistakes, be more sensitive to others when playing or singing in an ensemble, be more aware of intonation, improve your ability to memorise music and improve your ability to improvise and compose.

All the many elements of musical training are of course connected. So, when working through the activities in this book you will be connecting with many of them. You'll be listening, singing, clapping, playing your instrument, writing music down, improvising and composing – as well as developing that vital ability to do well at the aural tests in your grade exams!

Aural is not an occasional optional extra – just to be taken off a dusty shelf a few days (or even hours) before a music exam. It's something you can be developing and thinking about all the time. And as you go through the enjoyable and fun activities in these books you'll realise how important and useful having a good musical ear (being good at aural) really is.

How to use this book

When you have a few minutes to spare (perhaps at the beginning or end of a practice session), sit down with your instrument, by your CD player, and open this book. Choose a section and then work through the activities – you needn't do much each time. But whatever you do, do it carefully, repeating any activity if you feel it will help. In fact many of the activities will be fun to do again and again. And make sure that you come back to the book on a regular basis.

So, good luck and enjoy improving your aural skills!

Paul Harris and John Lenehan

For U.S. readers:
Bar   = Measure
Note = Tone
Tone = Whole step

Section 1 Pulse

Pulse is the heartbeat of music. It divides time into regular and equal units. Go for a walk taking short, even and regular steps. Listen to a clock ticking or watch a pendulum swinging; listen to a washing machine or a dishwasher – these are all examples of pulse.

● Pulse is all around us. How many other kinds of pulse can you think of?

● This is a steady pulse. Walk round the room (or on the spot) to the pulse. After you've finished listening to the track, continue to hear the pulse in your head.

Pulse can be grouped into patterns of two or more. (Each individual pulse is normally called a beat).

● This is a pulse in 2-time. Clap along with it.

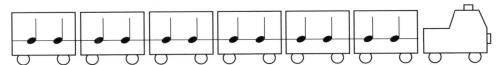

● This is a pulse in 3-time. Clap along with it.

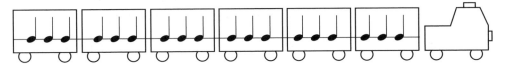

When writing music down, each group is divided by a bar-line and the space between each bar-line is called a bar.

● Put in the bar-lines:

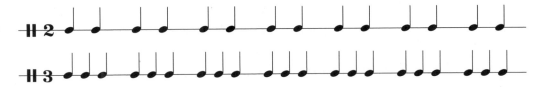

listening activities

track 5 **1** Clap along with the pulse, joining in as soon as you can. From time to time the pulse on the recording will stop. Keep going steadily and evenly all the time, until you hear the whistle.

track 6 **2** This time, instead of clapping the pulse out loud, hear it in your head.

track 7 **3** In this example, there is a lot more silence. Continue clapping the pulse throughout the track. Are you precisely with the pulse each time it returns?

track 8 **4** This time hear the pulse in your head. Are you precisely with the pulse each time it returns?

track 9 **5** In this exercise the pulse is 4-in-a-bar. After two introductory bars, one beat in each bar is missed out (the same one each time). Clap only the missing beat. Which beat is it?

track 10 **6** Here's a similar exercise but this time in 3-in-a-bar. Again clap the missing beat. Which beat is it?

track 11 **7** Here's an exercise to help you develop your own inner sense of pulse. You'll hear three bars of a pulse in 2-time with counting, and then it will stop. Continue counting on your own and silently in your head. In which bar and on which beat does the sound occur? What is the sound?

track 12 **8** Here's a similar example in 3-time. In which bar and on which beat does the sound occur? This time the sound is played by an instrument. Can you tell which one?

track 13 **9** Here are four examples of music in 2-time. Clap (or tap) the pulse, joining in as soon as you can.

track 14 **10** Here are four more examples, now in 3-time. Again, clap (or tap) the pulse, joining in as soon as you can.

track 15 **11** Clap (or tap) the pulse of each of the musical excerpts on this track, joining in as soon as you can. After each one, write down whether it was in 2-time or 3-time.

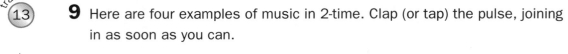

1 _____   2 _____   3 _____   4 _____   5 _____

track 16

12 In this exercise you'll hear a series of short rhythmic phrases in 2-time over a steady pulse. Clap or tap each one back straight away like an echo. The first one is done for you.

track 17

13 Here are some more exercises, now in 3-time. Again the first one is done for you.

track 18

14 This time, instead of repeating the rhythm, improvise your own rhythmic responses.

track 19

15 Listen to the phrase which will be repeated four times. Write down the rhythm on the line below:

$\parallel \frac{2}{4}$ _____|_____ $\parallel$

track 20

16 Now here's an example in 3-time. Listen to the phrase (repeated four times) and then write down the rhythm:

$\parallel \frac{3}{4}$ _____|_____ $\parallel$

17 Ask your teacher to play you one of the pieces you are learning. Clap or tap the pulse. How many beats in the bar?

18 Using a piece you are currently working on, hear the first four bars in your head. Now, without the music, have a go at answering the following questions:

- How many beats are there in each bar? _____
- What are the time values of the first two notes of the tune? _____
- Are there any rests in the first four bars? _____
- If so, what are they? _____
- Hear the first four bars in your head and at the same time tap the pulse.
- Now hear the pulse in your head and tap the rhythm.
- Write down the rhythm of the melody of the first four bars. Put in the time signature:

$\parallel$ _____|_____|_____|_____ $\parallel$

Come back and repeat this exercise using other pieces or using other four-bar phrases from the same piece.

Section 2 — Pitch

- Sing the highest note you can (comfortably) – and now the lowest. Now sing some of the notes in between.

Each of these notes is a different 'pitch'. Pitch is how high or low a sound seems. Some notes are 'high-pitched' and others are 'low-pitched'.

- Go to a piano or electric keyboard (or use your instrument if you don't have access to one of these) and sing a comfortable high note. Now try to find it on the instrument. Now do the same with a low note. How far apart are your highest and lowest notes? Is it more than one octave?

Like pulse, pitch is also all around us. Can you think of some high- and low-pitched animal sounds? For example, birdsong is usually high in pitch and a lion's roar is quite low in pitch. How would you describe the pitch of the following?

- A door creaking

- Your door bell

- The ringtone of your phone

- A car engine

Now listen to the three pieces on track 21. One is high-pitched (H), one medium- (M) and one low- (L). Put them in the correct order.

1 _____ 2 _____ 3 _____

Getting to know your voice

- Play a note on the piano (or on your instrument) in the middle of your range. Listen to it very carefully and then hear it in your head like a gentle hum.

- Now hear the hum get louder, still in your head. Now begin to hum the note out loud very quietly. Gradually get louder. You've successfully pitched a note. Repeat this many times using different notes.

- Now play two next-door notes, one after the other. Hear them in your head and then hum or sing them out loud to *lah* or any other sound. Repeat this many times using different pairs of notes.

- Sing a phrase from a piece you are studying. Get into the habit of singing, at least a few notes, every day.

listening activities

track 22 **1** A series of notes can move in three different ways – they can stay the same, go up or go down. On this track, you'll hear some two-note phrases. Some go up (U), some go down (D) and some stay the same (S). Now listen to the five phrases and write down the letters U, D or S after you've heard each one:

1 _____   2 _____   3 _____   4 _____   5 _____

track 23 **2** Now you'll hear the example again. This time you will be given longer pauses between each phrase for you to write the shape down. Here's how the first one should look:

1 _●_●___

2 _____   4 _____

3 _____   5 _____

track 24 **3** Here are the same notes again. This time sing each two-note pattern after you've heard it. The first one is sung for you.

track 25 **4** Now, with your instrument, play the notes after you've heard them. The first note is a concert C. Begin on any suitable octave. (B♭ instruments begin on D; E♭ instruments begin on A.)

track 26 **5** On this track there are five short phrases. Sing each phrase as soon as you've heard it. The first one is sung for you.

tracks 27-30 **6** On these four tracks you'll hear some more phrases. Follow the instructions on the CD.

7 Now have a go at making up your own short phrases using the notes C, D and E. Write them down, then hear them in your head, then sing them and then finally play them.

1   ═══════════════ ‖   2   ═══════════════ ‖

3   ═══════════════ ‖   4   ═══════════════ ‖

8 Working with a friend, try playing your tunes from the previous exercise. Ask your friend to sing and play them back to you.

tracks (31-36)

9 Here are some more short phrases. Sing each one back as soon as you've heard it.

10 Using a piece you are currently working on, find a suitable two-bar phrase and try to answer the following questions:

- How many different pitches are there in the phrase? _____
- Are any notes repeated? _____
- What is the name of the first note? _____
- Play the first note and then hear the phrase in your head.
- Now sing the phrase, firstly looking at the notes and then again from memory.
- Now, from memory, write the phrase down.

═══════════════════════════════ ‖

8

Section 3 Hearing changes

● Have a look at these pictures and try to spot the eight differences:

That wasn't too difficult! Hearing the difference between two musical phrases is not difficult either. You just have to be very awake because it has to be done from memory, and it all happens in a very short time.

● Cover up the right-hand picture below. Now look at the picture on the left and study it for about 30 seconds.

● Now swap – cover up the left-hand picture and study the one on the right. Try to spot the differences *without looking back at the first picture*.

Not quite so easy, because you have to really remember the first picture. This is similar to the way you have to think when hearing changes in musical phrases – it's all in the memory ...

listening activities

track
37

1 Clap the rhythm on this track.

2 Now write the rhythm down. The final note is given:

Now clap it from the music, counting the beats as you clap.

track
38

3 Now the phrase is repeated with a small alteration. Clap the new rhythm.

track
39

4 Now write it down:

Now try to describe the difference between the two.

_____

A good way to describe the change would be to say the first note was longer (or dotted) and the second note shorter. The rest of the music remained the same.

5 Now clap the original version again and then make up your own new version. Write it down here:

You'll notice that although the individual note values can change, the overall number of beats remains the same in each bar. So, just like in maths, music has to add up correctly.

6 Below you'll see a well-known carol. Firstly, reading the music, hear the piece through in your head. On the recording some bars have been changed. As you listen to the track, put a tick above the bars where a change has been made.

(Most changes will include one note being longer and therefore the next note will probably be shorter as a result. Occasionally it might be the other way round. For now, it is important just to hear in which bars the changes occur.)

7 On this track you'll hear a phrase played twice, with a change in the second version. Try to describe the change, bringing the position of the change into your answer. (For example, a good answer would be 'on the second playing the fourth note was longer' – but that's not it!)

The answer is revealed on track 42.

8 Make up your own pair of phrases, with a single change in the second phrase, and play them to a friend or your teacher. Can they spot the difference?

9 On these five tracks there are more similar examples. What was the difference between the phrases? Write your answers down and check them later.

10 Choose a passage from a piece you are currently learning and make some changes to the rhythm. Play the passage to your teacher and see whether they can spot the differences.

Section 4 Learning to listen to music

Learning to listen carefully to yourself and to other people playing music will help you improve your playing enormously. There are all sorts of features to listen out for, but for the Grade 1 exam you will only have to think about *dynamics* (loud and quiet playing) and *articulation* (smooth and detached playing).

From the moment you get up in the morning there will be many times when you hear music. Always take the opportunity to ask yourself some questions about it:

- Is the music loud (*forte*) or quiet (*piano*)?

- Is the music detached (*staccato*) or smooth (*legato*)?

- Does the music gradually get louder (*crescendo*) or quieter (*diminuendo*)?

- What instruments are playing?

listening activities

track **48** **1** As you listen to each of the three short pieces on this track, write down f (*forte*) for the loud sections and p (*piano*) for the quiet sections.

1 _____ _____

2 _____ _____ _____

3 _____ _____ _____ _____

track **49** **2** As you listen to each of the three short pieces on this track, write down L (*legato*) for the smooth sections and S (*staccato*) for the detached sections.

1 _____ _____

2 _____ _____ _____

3 _____ _____ _____

track **50** **3** Now write down $<$ (*crescendo*) or $>$ (*diminuendo*) as you hear them.

1 _____ _____

2 _____ _____

3 _____ _____

4 The next five tracks each contain a short piece. Each piece will be played twice. After the second playing, answer the following question:

track **51**
- Did the piece begin loudly?

  _____

track **52**
- Was the end louder than the start?

  _____

track **53**
- Was the smooth section at the beginning or the end?

  _____

track **54**
- Where was the detached playing?

  _____

track **55**
- Were the changes from quiet to loud sudden or gradual?

  _____

5 This time each piece is played only once and then you'll hear the questions:

track **56**
- _____

track **57**
- _____

track **58**
- _____

track **59**
- _____

track **60**
- _____

6 Using a piece you are currently working on, try the following*:

- Add more dynamic markings (in pencil) and perform the piece to your teacher. Can your teacher hear all your extra dynamics?

- Play the piece ignoring all the markings!

- Play the piece really exaggerating all the markings!

- Play the piece reversing all the dynamic markings (eg. $\boldsymbol{p} = \boldsymbol{f}$, *cresc.* = *dim.* etc.)

- Play the smooth sections staccato and the detached sections smoothly or, if the piece is mostly smooth, play it staccato and if it's mostly detached, play it all smoothly.

*See *Improve your practice!* Grade 1 for more activities like this

Section 5 # Making connections

These fun activities show you how aural connects with all the other aspects of music. Choose one or two each time you practise.

... with scales

Play the first note of a major scale you know well and then hear it in your head. Now play the scale very slowly, pre-hearing each note in your head *before* you play it.

... with tone quality

Listening to the *quality* of sound you make is very much part of aural. Choose a piece you are currently learning and play the first note (or, if it's a piano piece, the first chord or notes of both hands together) with the best tone quality you can.

... with intervals

Play a note and then, in your head, hear the note a tone (or major second) above (for example, play C and then hear D). Then play the note to see how accurate you were. Try to find some examples of tones in the pieces you are currently studying.

... with sight-reading

Choose a sight-reading piece* and try to hear it first in your head. Then play it.

... with memory

Choose a short phrase from a piece you are learning (two to four bars in length). Play it a few times, then, without the music, hear it in your head a few times and then play it from memory.

... with rhythm

Make up a four-bar rhythm in your head. Then write it down and clap it.

*For example from *Improve your sight-reading!* Grade 1

14

... with conducting

Listen to the theme tune to one of your favourite television programmes. What is the time signature? Ask your teacher how to beat time for that time signature and then conduct the music the next time you hear it.

... with music history

As a developing musician you will need to recognise the changing historical styles of music. Understanding style and musical periods will also help you to play your pieces with more conviction and authority. You'll hear four pieces, each from a different musical period. Using the descriptions, try to connect the boxes.

> **Baroque**
> Slow dance in $\frac{3}{4}$

> played 1st

> **Classical**
> Sonata movement with lots of scale patterns

> played 2nd

> **Romantic**
> Character piece describing a storm

> played 3rd

> **20th/21st century**
> Pop-style ballad

> played 4th

> Composer's name:

A final message from the authors!

Answers

(by CD track number)

Section 1: *Pulse*

9 Third beat

10 Second beat

11 Bar 9, second beat – telephone

12 Bar 8, second beat – church organ

15 1:3, 2:2, 3:2, 4:3, 5:2

19

20

Section 2: *Pitch*

21 1:M, 2:L, 3:H

22 1:U, 2:S, 3:D, 4:U, 5:S

Section 3: *Hearing changes*

37

38

40 Changes in bars 3, 5, 10, 11, 14, 16

43 The first note was longer

44 The note before last was longer (or the dotted rhythm was evened out)

45 The first note was shorter

46 The third note was longer (or there was a dotted rhythm at the end of the first bar)

47 The note before last was shorter (or there was a dotted rhythm at the beginning of the second bar)

Section 4: *Learning to listen to music*

48 1: p, f 2: p, f, p 3: f, p, f, p

49 1: L, S   2: S, L, S   3: L, S, L

50 1: $<\,>$ 2: $>\,<$ 3: $>\,<\,>$

51 No

52 Yes

53 End

54 End

55 Sudden

56 Yes/Middle

57 No/Beginning

58 Staccato/No (ended loudly)

59 End/No (began loudly)

60 Sudden/p

Section 5: *Making connections*

61 The composer was BACH

This book belongs to

Includes 2 each of 25 coloring images based on the scenes and characters of the Memory's Wake Trilogy, an illustrated young adult fantasy series by Selina Fenech.

As an artist, color is a thing of magic in my life. Color creates shapes, forms, and feelings in the artworks I paint. Laying color onto a blank page is when I feel closest to true magic, when I feel happiest and most relaxed, and it's through what I create that I share my love of magic with the world. Through my coloring books I want to share that same magic with you.

The artworks in my books are based on my designs from the fantasy trilogy I wrote and illustrated, Memory's Wake. With a modern heroine, a lost princess, a wild forest-man, a charming thief, a dragon, fairies, Arthurian mythology, and Victorian style, Memory's Wake is an exciting tale of magic, romance, and family love for all ages.

See more about the Memory's Wake Trilogy at www.selinafenech.com

Victorian Romance - The Memory's Wake Coloring Book
by Selina Fenech
First Published March 2017
Published by Fairies and Fantasy PTY LTD
ISBN: 978-0-6480269-1-4

Using This Book

Turn off and move away from distractions. Relax into the peaceful process of coloring and enjoy the magic of these fantasy images.

Experiment! There is no right or wrong way to color, and with two of each image, there's no pressure.

This book works best with color pencils or markers. Wet mediums should be used sparingly. Slip a piece of card behind the image you're working on in case the markers bleed through.

Don't be scared to dismantle this book. Cut finished pages out to frame, or split the book in half where the second set of images start so you and a loved one can color together.

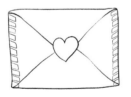

Never run out of fantasy coloring pages by signing up to Selina's newsletter. Get free downloadable pages and updates on new books at - selinafenech.com/free-coloring-sampler/

Share Your Work

Share on Instagram with #colorselina to be included in Selina's coloring gallery, and visit the gallery for inspiration.

selinafenech.com/coloringgallery

"Happily Ever After"

Memory stared over Eloryn's shoulder, where daylight brightened the diamond cut glass window of the balcony doors. Outside a thorny vine grew around the balustrade. The silhouette of a wild young man perched on it in front of the sun. She smiled. "Besides, things never just disappear. They have to go somewhere, right?"

Whatever else might still be wrong with me, wherever the lost parts of my broken soul are, for now at least I'm alive, can live, here with my family.

"Family"

"I know you're hurting. It would be insane if you weren't after everything you've been through. There's no quick fix, but I'll be there for you. And you will be there for me, too, like you always have."

"Kiss by Candlelight"

"It's not proper for me to voice my desires so. It's just… to have you so near, knowing you feel for me how I do for you, it's all I can do not to take you and hold you and do all sorts of delicious things with you." Roen bit his bottom lip and his smile returned.

Eloryn didn't think she could blush any harder, but she did. Her body turned to fire just wondering what delicious things Roen could mean. She didn't know what they were, but she knew she wanted them, and wanted him. She also couldn't help but wonder whether there had been other women in the past that he'd done such things with.

"You know I've never…" Eloryn began, but choked up. When her words returned, they came at rambling speed. "My first kiss was yours, and I know little else of love apart from the simple romance in fairytales and one archaic text book on anatomy and reproduction. I fear that love may be an area in which you are more knowledgeable than I."

"Whatever experiences I've had, they weren't of love. You are my first experience of love." Roen took both her hands in one of his, and the warm light of the lamp he held beside them seemed to make them glow. "I don't expect you to act at all outside of your comfort, or of society's standards. I would never think to pressure you further. I simply want you to understand how desirable I find you. How strong, and brave, and kind you are."

"The Raid"

The carriage sped through the empty streets of Caermaellan. Over the clatter of the wheels and hooves on cobblestones, Memory heard a nearby clock tower ring for two in the morning. She could also hear the dozen or so guards on horseback escorting them. More empty coaches, larger and slower than the sleek model Memory rode in, were driven behind, in the hopes there would be survivors to bring home.

It had felt like a lifetime since Memory had driven these streets, distant days of going to school or visiting her homeless shelter, or her night with Dylan where he compared her to the moon. Memory wondered where he was now and wondered when her life would slow down enough to go back to school again, to continue her magic classes with Bedevere, to continue with her life.

When the lives of those I love are also safe. That's when.

"Hope"

She looked out across the tree tops. The rain had stopped, but the trees still sparkled in the moonlight. Flashes of darting sprites matched the shining leaves. She thought she could hear singing, somewhere distant, mingling with the sounds of night. A bittersweet song with a strange melody, somehow familiar.

"*Forever*"

"Don't you want… can I still be by your side?"

Memory drew a trembling breath. She felt all of her seventeen years old, staring up at the most beautiful boy in the world. "I do. I mean, if it's what you want. Not for anything you feel you owe me. Only if you want to. Only if you want… me."

Will's gaze stole straight into her soul as he bent his face to hers. "I want you."

"Rest"

The atmosphere in this room made her chest tight. It was so much, too much, like Alward's library at home. Alward, like Lucan, had lovingly filled every space with books for them and their students. From ancient illuminated tomes to newer press printed collections and Alward's own studies, hand bound and hand written.

The monastery had an extensive library even before Alward arrived. She only had the faintest recollections of the people of the old religion who hid her in her earliest days. Their order valued secrecy on certain subjects, like that of men arriving with motherless children. The old men and women were faded memories by the time she was reading their books.

Eloryn closed her eyes. Leaning back into the armchair, she wondered if those books were still there. After the last of the priests passed away, it was only ever her, Alward, and the books. Often all three together, when she was still small enough to curl up in a chair with Alward and be read to.

I miss him. I miss those books. I even miss the high stone walls.

"The Great Fight for Everyone"

The dragon blinked huge verdant eyes. "I have been watching you since you came to our realm."

Memory winced, both for the power of the dragon's voice in her head, and for her failures the dragon must have observed.

Will spoke, obviously hearing everything Memory heard. "Why? What do you want?"

"I am trying to decide what it is you are doing. If you mean to harm or help the fae as we draw to our end."

"I'm just here to save my friends. Standard search and rescue then we're going home. I wasn't even thinking about…" *I wasn't even thinking about anyone else.* Memory let out a breath like she'd taken a baseball bat to the chest. *My friends are in trouble, and I wasn't even thinking about anyone else.*

Memory took a step closer to the dragon. His scales were patchy, missing in places, moldering. "Dragon, are you dying?"

"Seelie Queen Aine"

Although Aine's face was turned to the side, Memory could see the seelie queen's eyes tracking her as she crossed the floor to stand below the throne. The fairy's long hair tumbled like living bronze down from her high perch, all the way to the floor, and swished when she shifted position to address Memory. Her gown seemed to be made of the same type of cobwebs Shonae had been collecting, woven into a tight fitting, barely-there slip that dangled around her, the tattered tips ringing with small bells. She was impossibly beautiful.

"Caught in a Fairy Ring"

"Would you call a snake or spider evil? They are creatures of nature, same as the unseelie, same as all fae, same as humans. We are as we are and all have our place in the balance."

"Charming Thief"

"Would you still be here with me now, if I was never a princess?" Eloryn's tone became cold.

Roen's voice came up short, breaking before a word could come out. He forced the words through. "I didn't know you were a princess when I returned your bag that day."

Despite the words spoken being true, Roen cursed himself as a liar. He wouldn't have been here, now, if he hadn't seen that medallion, hadn't known with one look. He wouldn't have put himself at risk to hide them from the guards. And if that hadn't ended badly, he simply would have used her, like he did other women, and then forgotten her. That was the reality of who he was; criminal, philanderer, sparkless seventh son of a seventh son. A man who had no place by her side.

"Worlds Can't Keep Us Apart"

"I don't want to be scared anymore. For you, and for me, I don't want to be scared to live my life. And I want to live my life with you. Whatever the rules, whatever might happen, I don't ever want to be apart from you again."

"Worlds couldn't keep us apart," Memory replied. "Tried and failed already."

"For You"

"You are everything a princess should be: kind, clever, brave, beautiful. If I behave differently for you, it's only because whatever I was, whatever I am, I need to be better for you."

"Fairy Encounter"

The sprite hovered just above the water, her pointed toes occasionally dipping in and causing ripples. There was an almost faded quality to the way that she looked, translucent and glowing like milky glass lit from behind. Her flame red hair, the one splash of color on her, lifted and swirled around a pretty face marred by a scowl.

"Stolen Kiss"

"I love you in a way that should make me a poet, but instead leaves me speechless."

"Dark Mirror"

"I'm you. And you're me. The broken pieces of our self." She looked at Memory, a vacant, sad look in her eyes. "I'm here to be with you. Nobody can ever like us and nobody else will ever understand. Those idiots won't take long to figure out you're not a whole, real person. What do you think they'll do when they realize the monster you are? Still pretend to be your friend?"

"Missing You"

"I feel I'm making so many mistakes. I owe the Council my trust and loyalty, but find my trust given to men with misogynistic, antiquated, hard-line views. And even knowing that, I've handed so much power to them because I couldn't use that power myself. I'm just not a ruler. But I'm worried. So worried that I've done the wrong thing. I don't know if I can keep going along with their wishes, but don't know how to challenge them."

Eloryn pulled back. She dried her face with a handkerchief but desperation still filled her voice. "What if you try your hardest to be strong, and do your duty, but it's simply not who you are?"

"My Sweet Pet"

"My sweet pet," she sang, and twirled around him, dancing as he ate. She had delicate, tattered wings which trailed a stream of glittery light behind them. Will ate and ate. Mina sang and smiled. He thought he'd received a miracle. He thought he was saved. He had no idea what had just happened. His life had become the property of the fairy before him.

"A New World"

Memory hopped down from the carriage, wanting to run off in every direction at once. The city was so enticing, full of misty secrets and winding pathways to explore.

"Providence Unveiled"

They tell me my name is Memory.
They tell me that I did amazing things.
They tell me all about this land I'm in and the changes that
are happening here.

"Hope's Reign"

"You think you're making friends here. You think you're starting a new life. But eventually they'll all turn on you or leave you. Every last one. Trust me. I'm the only one here for you. You think they like you? How could they? They don't know you. You don't know you. You're not even a whole person."

"At the Masque"

Memory stood still, shell shocked. Rough hands grabbed her from behind. One forceful tug pulled her back into the scratching leaves of the hedge.

She tried to wriggle free, but strong arms pinned her against a body of firm muscles and furs. Dragged through the dense foliage, she closed her eyes to the twigs that rushed by. In a burst of leaves, she and her abductor emerged from the hedge. She looked up into blue eyes. Blue like the sea, they even made her feel sea-sick looking into them. Eyes she remembered from the forest.

"Studying"

The book lay open on the floor, its ruffled pages showing an intricate illustration of a majestic sword. *Oh, pretty.*

Memory picked the book up and drifted across to the armchair in the corner, staring at the sword. The caption called it Caliburn, sword of Arthur Maellan. Memory wondered if he might be one of her ancestors. Memory flicked to the next page, skimming over the text, hungry for more information.

"Who We Once Were"

"I have loved you so long. Since the day you saved me until this day. I've fallen in love with you over and over. I loved who you were. I loved who I remembered you were. Then I loved who you became."

"Because of You"

"Back at Elder's Bridge inn, when I'd been caught and called out, I had been ready to die. I told you and Mem what I really was because I wanted you to hate me like I hated myself. I wanted you to leave me there to my fate. At the time, I thought I deserved it."

Eloryn's head shook in fierce denial.

Roen continued. "Today, I could only think about how much I needed to live. Even if everyone knows the truth of my past. It seems as though at some point I have stopped hating myself. I don't know when, or how, but I suspect it has more than a little to do with you."

Second Set of Pages Begins Here

When designing my books I decided to print them with two copies of each design, because as an artist I know there are always so many possibilities! I also wanted to give everybody the chance of a do-over with every design in case of an oops (as an artist I know that happens too!). Try a different medium, or a different colour scheme. Create without fear! Or share the magic with a loved one. Because sharing your creativity and joy of color is the best magic of all. ~ *Selina*

"Happily Ever After"

Memory stared over Eloryn's shoulder, where daylight brightened the diamond cut glass window of the balcony doors. Outside a thorny vine grew around the balustrade. The silhouette of a wild young man perched on it in front of the sun. She smiled. "Besides, things never just disappear. They have to go somewhere, right?"

Whatever else might still be wrong with me, wherever the lost parts of my broken soul are, for now at least I'm alive, can live, here with my family.

"Family"

"I know you're hurting. It would be insane if you weren't after everything you've been through. There's no quick fix, but I'll be there for you. And you will be there for me, too, like you always have."

"Kiss by Candlelight"

"It's not proper for me to voice my desires so. It's just… to have you so near, knowing you feel for me how I do for you, it's all I can do not to take you and hold you and do all sorts of delicious things with you." Roen bit his bottom lip and his smile returned.

Eloryn didn't think she could blush any harder, but she did. Her body turned to fire just wondering what delicious things Roen could mean. She didn't know what they were, but she knew she wanted them, and wanted him. She also couldn't help but wonder whether there had been other women in the past that he'd done such things with.

"You know I've never…" Eloryn began, but choked up. When her words returned, they came at rambling speed. "My first kiss was yours, and I know little else of love apart from the simple romance in fairytales and one archaic text book on anatomy and reproduction. I fear that love may be an area in which you are more knowledgeable than I."

"Whatever experiences I've had, they weren't of love. You are my first experience of love." Roen took both her hands in one of his, and the warm light of the lamp he held beside them seemed to make them glow. "I don't expect you to act at all outside of your comfort, or of society's standards. I would never think to pressure you further. I simply want you to understand how desirable I find you. How strong, and brave, and kind you are."

"The Raid"

The carriage sped through the empty streets of Caermaellan. Over the clatter of the wheels and hooves on cobblestones, Memory heard a nearby clock tower ring for two in the morning. She could also hear the dozen or so guards on horseback escorting them. More empty coaches, larger and slower than the sleek model Memory rode in, were driven behind, in the hopes there would be survivors to bring home.

It had felt like a lifetime since Memory had driven these streets, distant days of going to school or visiting her homeless shelter, or her night with Dylan where he compared her to the moon. Memory wondered where he was now and wondered when her life would slow down enough to go back to school again, to continue her magic classes with Bedevere, to continue with her life.

When the lives of those I love are also safe. That's when.

"Hope"

She looked out across the tree tops. The rain had stopped, but the trees still sparkled in the moonlight. Flashes of darting sprites matched the shining leaves. She thought she could hear singing, somewhere distant, mingling with the sounds of night. A bittersweet song with a strange melody, somehow familiar.

"Forever"

"Don't you want… can I still be by your side?"

Memory drew a trembling breath. She felt all of her seventeen years old, staring up at the most beautiful boy in the world. "I do. I mean, if it's what you want. Not for anything you feel you owe me. Only if you want to. Only if you want… me."

Will's gaze stole straight into her soul as he bent his face to hers. "I want you."

"Rest"

The atmosphere in this room made her chest tight. It was so much, too much, like Alward's library at home. Alward, like Lucan, had lovingly filled every space with books for them and their students. From ancient illuminated tomes to newer press printed collections and Alward's own studies, hand bound and hand written.

The monastery had an extensive library even before Alward arrived. She only had the faintest recollections of the people of the old religion who hid her in her earliest days. Their order valued secrecy on certain subjects, like that of men arriving with motherless children. The old men and women were faded memories by the time she was reading their books.

Eloryn closed her eyes. Leaning back into the armchair, she wondered if those books were still there. After the last of the priests passed away, it was only ever her, Alward, and the books. Often all three together, when she was still small enough to curl up in a chair with Alward and be read to.

I miss him. I miss those books. I even miss the high stone walls.

"The Great Fight for Everyone"

The dragon blinked huge verdant eyes. "I have been watching you since you came to our realm."

Memory winced, both for the power of the dragon's voice in her head, and for her failures the dragon must have observed.

Will spoke, obviously hearing everything Memory heard. "Why? What do you want?"

"I am trying to decide what it is you are doing. If you mean to harm or help the fae as we draw to our end."

"I'm just here to save my friends. Standard search and rescue then we're going home. I wasn't even thinking about…" *I wasn't even thinking about anyone else.* Memory let out a breath like she'd taken a baseball bat to the chest. *My friends are in trouble, and I wasn't even thinking about anyone else.*

Memory took a step closer to the dragon. His scales were patchy, missing in places, moldering. "Dragon, are you dying?"

"Seelie Queen Aine"

Although Aine's face was turned to the side, Memory could see the seelie queen's eyes tracking her as she crossed the floor to stand below the throne. The fairy's long hair tumbled like living bronze down from her high perch, all the way to the floor, and swished when she shifted position to address Memory. Her gown seemed to be made of the same type of cobwebs Shonae had been collecting, woven into a tight fitting, barely-there slip that dangled around her, the tattered tips ringing with small bells. She was impossibly beautiful.

"Caught in a Fairy Ring"

"Would you call a snake or spider evil? They are creatures of nature, same as
the unseelie, same as all fae, same as humans. We are as we are and all have our
place in the balance."

"Charming Thief"

"Would you still be here with me now, if I was never a princess?" Eloryn's tone became cold.

Roen's voice came up short, breaking before a word could come out. He forced the words through. "I didn't know you were a princess when I returned your bag that day."

Despite the words spoken being true, Roen cursed himself as a liar. He wouldn't have been here, now, if he hadn't seen that medallion, hadn't known with one look. He wouldn't have put himself at risk to hide them from the guards. And if that hadn't ended badly, he simply would have used her, like he did other women, and then forgotten her. That was the reality of who he was; criminal, philanderer, sparkless seventh son of a seventh son. A man who had no place by her side.

"Worlds Can't Keep Us Apart"

"I don't want to be scared anymore. For you, and for me, I don't want to be scared to live my life. And I want to live my life with you. Whatever the rules, whatever might happen, I don't ever want to be apart from you again."

"Worlds couldn't keep us apart," Memory replied. "Tried and failed already."

"For You"

"You are everything a princess should be: kind, clever, brave, beautiful. If I behave differently for you, it's only because whatever I was, whatever I am, I need to be better for you."

"Fairy Encounter"

The sprite hovered just above the water, her pointed toes occasionally dipping in and causing ripples. There was an almost faded quality to the way that she looked, translucent and glowing like milky glass lit from behind. Her flame red hair, the one splash of color on her, lifted and swirled around a pretty face marred by a scowl.

"Stolen Kiss"

"I love you in a way that should make me a poet, but instead leaves me speechless."

"Dark Mirror"

"I'm you. And you're me. The broken pieces of our self." She looked at Memory, a vacant, sad look in her eyes. "I'm here to be with you. Nobody can ever like us and nobody else will ever understand. Those idiots won't take long to figure out you're not a whole, real person. What do you think they'll do when they realize the monster you are? Still pretend to be your friend?"

"Missing You"

"I feel I'm making so many mistakes. I owe the Council my trust and loyalty, but find my trust given to men with misogynistic, antiquated, hard-line views. And even knowing that, I've handed so much power to them because I couldn't use that power myself. I'm just not a ruler. But I'm worried. So worried that I've done the wrong thing. I don't know if I can keep going along with their wishes, but don't know how to challenge them."

Eloryn pulled back. She dried her face with a handkerchief but desperation still filled her voice. "What if you try your hardest to be strong, and do your duty, but it's simply not who you are?"

"My Sweet Pet"

"My sweet pet," she sang, and twirled around him, dancing as he ate. She had delicate, tattered wings which trailed a stream of glittery light behind them. Will ate and ate. Mina sang and smiled. He thought he'd received a miracle. He thought he was saved. He had no idea what had just happened. His life had become the property of the fairy before him.

"A New World"

Memory hopped down from the carriage, wanting to run off in every direction at once. The city was so enticing, full of misty secrets and winding pathways to explore.

"Providence Unveiled"

They tell me my name is Memory.
They tell me that I did amazing things.
They tell me all about this land I'm in and the changes that
are happening here.

"Hope's Reign"

"You think you're making friends here. You think you're starting a new life. But eventually they'll all turn on you or leave you. Every last one. Trust me. I'm the only one here for you. You think they like you? How could they? They don't know you. You don't know you. You're not even a whole person."

"At the Masque"

Memory stood still, shell shocked. Rough hands grabbed her from behind. One forceful tug pulled her back into the scratching leaves of the hedge.

She tried to wriggle free, but strong arms pinned her against a body of firm muscles and furs. Dragged through the dense foliage, she closed her eyes to the twigs that rushed by. In a burst of leaves, she and her abductor emerged from the hedge. She looked up into blue eyes. Blue like the sea, they even made her feel seasick looking into them. Eyes she remembered from the forest.

"Studying"

The book lay open on the floor, its ruffled pages showing an intricate illustration of a majestic sword. *Oh, pretty.*

Memory picked the book up and drifted across to the armchair in the corner, staring at the sword. The caption called it Caliburn, sword of Arthur Maellan. Memory wondered if he might be one of her ancestors. Memory flicked to the next page, skimming over the text, hungry for more information.

"Who We Once Were"

"I have loved you so long. Since the day you saved me until this day. I've fallen in love with you over and over. I loved who you were. I loved who I remembered you were. Then I loved who you became."

"Because of You"

"Back at Elder's Bridge inn, when I'd been caught and called out, I had been ready to die. I told you and Mem what I really was because I wanted you to hate me like I hated myself. I wanted you to leave me there to my fate. At the time, I thought I deserved it."

Eloryn's head shook in fierce denial.

Roen continued. "Today, I could only think about how much I needed to live. Even if everyone knows the truth of my past. It seems as though at some point I have stopped hating myself. I don't know when, or how, but I suspect it has more than a little to do with you."

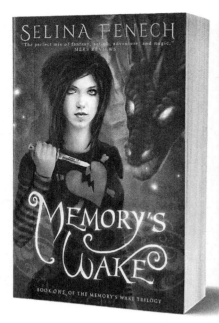  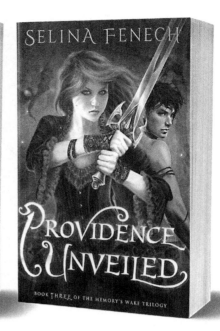

I don't know who I am. I don't know what I am.
All I know is that I'm being hunted, and this world is not my own.

Lost and hunted in a land of magic and monstrous fairies, a trouble teen has to find out why her memories were stolen before she is found by those who want her dead. Paperback, eBook, and Audio Editions plus Omnibus and Companion Guide.

About the Artist and Author

As a lover of all things fantasy, Selina has made a living as an artist since she was 23 years old selling her magical creations. Her works range from oil paintings to oracle decks, dolls to digital scrapbooking, plus Young Adult novels, jewelry, and coloring books.

Born in 1981 to Australian and Maltese parents, Selina lives in Australia with her husband, daughter, and growing urban farm menagerie.

See all books online at viewauthor.at/sfcolor

Printed in Great Britain
by Amazon

20074699R00061